Collins

Easy Learning

Handwriting
Age 5-7

My name is _____ .

I am _____ years old.

I go to _____ School.

My favourite book is _____ _____ .

How to use this book

- Find a quiet, comfortable place to work, away from other distractions.

- Tackle one topic at a time.

- Help with reading the instructions where necessary, and ensure that your child understands what to do.

- Help and encourage your child to check their handwriting as they complete each activity.

- Discuss with your child what they have learnt.

- Let your child return to their favourite pages once they have been completed, to talk about the activities.

- Reward your child with plenty of praise and encouragement.

- Please note that some schools use different handwriting styles to this book. Check which style your child's school uses.

Special features

Yellow boxes: Introduce and outline the key handwriting ideas.

Published by Collins
An imprint of HarperCollinsPublishers
77–85 Fulham Palace Road
Hammersmith
London
W6 8JB

Browse the complete Collins catalogue at
www.collins.co.uk

First published in 2006
© HarperCollinsPublishers Limited 2008

10 9 8 7 6 5 4 3

ISBN -13 978-0-00-730103-4

British Library Cataloguing in Publication Data
A Catalogue record for this publication is available from the British Library

Design and layout by Graham M Brasnett
Illustrated by Andy Tudor
Cover design by Susi Martin
Cover illustration by John Haslam
Printed and bound in China

Contents

Small letters

Trace and write.

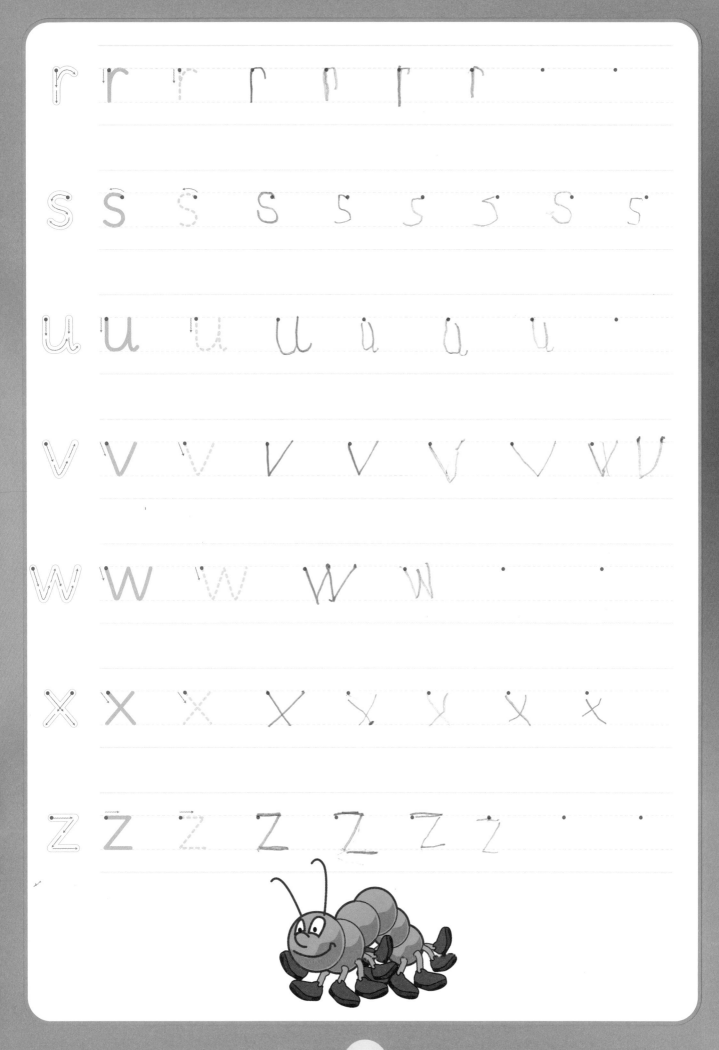

Tall letters

Trace and write.

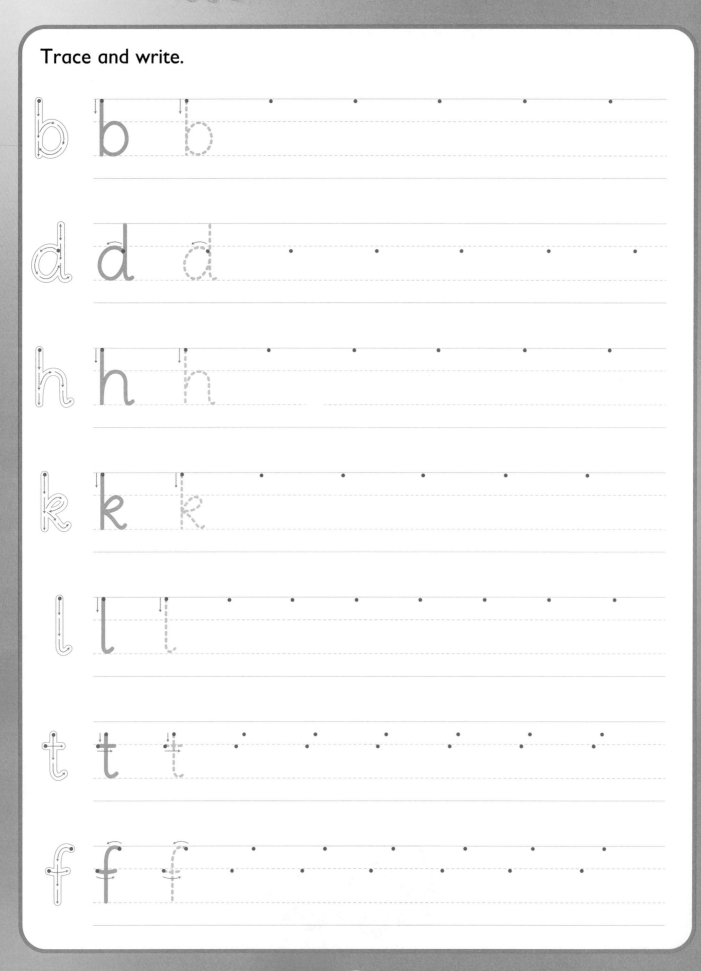

Trace and write.

g g g · · · · ·

j j j · · · · · · ·

p p p · · · · ·

q q q · · · · ·

y y y · · · ·

Trace the letters. Start at the red dot and follow the arrows.

Trace and write.

in   in

mp   mp

ly   ly

tr   tr

dr   dr

Trace and write.

 bin   bin

 jam   jam

 pen   pen

 bun   bun

 zip   zip

 pin   pin

yummy in my
tummy

yummy in my

tummy

Trace the letters. Start at the red dot and follow the arrows.

Trace and write.

it   it   ·   ·   ·   ·   ·   ·   ·   ·   ·   ·

al   al   ·   ·   ·   ·   ·   ·

nk   nk   ·   ·   ·   ·   ·   ·

lt   lt   ·   ·   ·   ·   ·   ·   ·   ·   ·   ·   ·   ·

cl   cl   ·   ·   ·   ·   ·   ·

Trace and write.

ball   ball

hit   hit

bat   bat

bell   bell

hut   hut

pull   pull

I like the pink kite
I like the pink kite

Trace the letters. Start at the red dot and follow the arrows. Remember to go to the top of the letter o, stop, and back round to the left.

Trace and write.

do   do

ug   ug

ea   ea

ld   ld

nd   nd

Trace and write.

 bed bed

 cap cap

 bag bag

 cake cake

 hand hand

 banana banana

dad's mad if my
cat's bad

dad's mad if my
cat's bad

Trace the letters. Start at the red dot and follow the arrows.

Trace and write.

ou   ou   ·   ·   ·

ri   ri   ·   ·   ·

vy   vy   ·   ·   ·

fr   fr   ·   ·   ·   ·

wi   wi   ·   ·   ·

Trace and write.

 wig wig

 boy boy

 one one

 ring ring

 home home

 love love

a mouse in the house

a mouse in the house

Trace the letters. Start at the red dot and follow the arrows.

Trace and write.

ot   ot   ·   ·   ·   ·

of   of   ·   ·   ·   ·

rt   rt   ·   ·   ·   ·

fl   fl   ·   ·   ·   ·   ·

ft   ft   ·   ·   ·   ·

Trace and write.

 owl owl

 hole hole

 knot knot

 book book

 whale whale

 school school

oh no, a mole in
a hole

oh no, a mole in
a hole

17

The sixth join

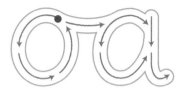

Trace the letters. Start at the red dot and follow the arrows. Remember to go to the top of the letter a, stop, and back round to the left.

Trace and write.

oa oa · · ·

vo vo · · ·

og og · · ·

ad ad · · ·

uc uc · · ·

Trace and write.

 dog   dog

 frog   frog

 wood   wood

 door   door

 sock   sock

 water   water

a toad in the road

a toad in the road

ch and sh

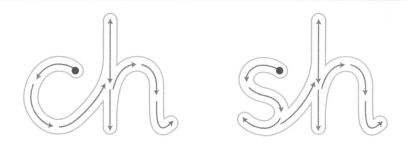

These pairs of letters are often seen together at the beginning and end of words. They are also good examples of the second join. Trace the letters.

Trace and write.

chair   child   arch

munch, crunch, chips for lunch

Trace and write.

shoe   shop   dish

splish, splash, the sheep had a wash

th wh

These pairs of letters are often seen together at the beginning of words. Th is also seen at the end of words too. Trace the letters.

Trace and write.

three   thumb   month

I think my brother has big teeth

Trace and write.

who   what   white

where, oh where, is my bear?

e, f and s

These three letters are tricky ones! Trace the letters. Now let's look at how they join to and from other letters.

Trace and write.

ee   ee

end   end

elephant   elephant

three   three

bears sleep easy
when it's breezy

22

Trace and write.

first first

after after

off off

the fly flew off

after the frog

Trace and write.

sun sun

crows crows

hiss hiss

scary snakes slide

and hiss

Break letters

These letters are break letters. They don't join to any other letter.

b g j p q x y z

Trace and write.

brother   brother

girl   girl

jump   jump

people   people

queen   queen

xylophone   xylophone

young   young

zebra   zebra

zebras jump over
purple boxes

Capital letters

Capital letters are similar to break letters. They don't join to any other letter.

Trace and write.

A A   B B   C C

D D   E E   F F

G G   H H   I I

J J   K K   L L

M M   N N   O O

P P   Q Q   R R

S S   T T   U U

V V   W W   X X

Y Y   Z Z

Days of the week

Trace and write.

Monday

Tuesday

Wednesday

Thursday

Friday

Saturday

Sunday

Trace and write.

1   one   1   one

2   two

3   three   three

4   four   3 3

5   five

6   six   six

7   seven

8   eight

9   nine

10   ten

11   eleven

12   twelve

13   thirteen

14   fourteen

15   fifteen

16   sixteen

17   seventeen

18   eighteen

19   nineteen

20   twenty

Colours

Trace and write.

red

blue

green

yellow

pink

purple

orange

brown

white

Writing an invitation

In your best handwriting, write to a friend and invite them to your birthday party.

Dear _____

You are invited to my birthday party

on _____

From _____

In your best handwriting, write a letter to thank someone in your family for a present. Put your address and the date at the top.

_____

_____

_____

_____

Dear_____

_____

_____

_____

_____

_____

_____

Love_____